Flavoring with Culi

Also by Mary El-Baz

Easy and Healthful Mediterranean Cooking

Building a Healthy Lifestyle: A Simple Nutrition and Fitness Approach

Flavoring with Culinary Herbs

◆

Tips, Recipes, and Cultivation

Mary El-Baz

iUniverse, Inc.
New York Lincoln Shanghai

Flavoring with Culinary Herbs
Tips, Recipes, and Cultivation

Copyright © 2005 by Mary El-Baz

All rights reserved. No part of this book may be used or reproduced by any means, graphic, electronic, or mechanical, including photocopying, recording, taping or by any information storage retrieval system without the written permission of the publisher except in the case of brief quotations embodied in critical articles and reviews.

iUniverse books may be ordered through booksellers or by contacting:

iUniverse
2021 Pine Lake Road, Suite 100
Lincoln, NE 68512
www.iuniverse.com
1-800-Authors (1-800-288-4677)

ISBN-13: 978-0-595-37936-1 (pbk)
ISBN-13: 978-0-595-82306-2 (ebk)
ISBN-10: 0-595-37936-2 (pbk)
ISBN-10: 0-595-82306-8 (ebk)

Printed in the United States of America

—To my family and friends who delight in the bouquet and flavor of savory cuisine

Contents

Savor the Flavor of Culinary Herbs! 1
Herbs That Blend With Certain Foods 4
    Herbs for Breads 4
    Herbs for Cheeses 4
    Herbs for Vegetables 4
    Herbs for Fruits and Sweets 4
    Herbs for Salad Dressings and Salads 5
    Herbs for Soups 5
    Herbs for Meats, Poultry, Fish, and Eggs 5
    Herbs for Beverages 6
Cooking with Herbs 7
    • *Pungent* 8
        Rosemary 8
            Rosemary Chicken in Mushroom Sauce 8
            Rosemary Focaccia 9
        Sage 10
            Gnocchi with Fried Sage Leaves 10
            Sage Drop Biscuits 11
            Stuffed Mushrooms with Sage 11
        Winter Savory 12
            Beef Pot Roast 13
            Ham and Bean Soup 14
            Savory Roasted Potatoes 14
    • *Strongly Accented* 15
        Basil 15
            Basil Pesto 16
            Tomato-Basil-Mozzarella Salad 16

Flavoring with Culinary Herbs

Cilantro and Coriander 17
   Lemon-Coriander Tea Cookies *17*
   Salsa Verde *18*
   Steak Seasoning *19*
   Thai Shrimp with Pasta *19*
Dill 20
   Cucumbers in Sour Cream *21*
   Dill Batter Bread *21*
   Dill Mayonnaise *22*
Mints—Spearmint and Peppermint 22
   Fresh Persimmons and Mint *23*
   Moroccan Mint Tea *23*
   Peppermint Soda *24*
Tarragon 24
   Beets with Tarragon *25*
   Tarragon Turkey Breast *26*
   Tarragon Vinegar *26*
Thyme 27
   Chicken Noodle Soup with Thyme *27*
   Soft Cheese Spread with Thyme *28*

- *Mixers* *28*

Chervil 28
   Chervil Pesto Spread *29*
   Cream of Broccoli and Chervil Soup *29*
Chives 30
   Baked Flounder with Chives *31*
   Chives and Cream Cheese Spread *31*
Parsley 31
   Parsley Crumb-Topped Tomatoes *32*
   Tabbouleh *32*
Summer Savory 33
   Green Bean and Baby Swiss Salad *33*
   Grilled Pork Chops with Summer Savory-Mustard Marinade *34*
Oregano 34
   Black Olive Tapanade *35*
   Herbed Angel Hair Pasta *35*

Contents   ix

    Marjoram; Sweet, Pot, and Wild 36
        Asparagus Salad with Balsamic Vinegar *37*
        Multi-Purpose Beef Blend *37*

Herb Substitutions 39

Herb Butter 40
    Lemon-Tarragon Butter *40*
    Parsley Butter *41*
    Sage-Thyme Butter *41*

Herb Seasoning Blends 42
    Fines Herbes *42*
    Herbes de Provence *42*
    Fresh Bouquet Garni *43*
    Dried Bouquet Garni *43*

Herb Cordials 45
    Basic Herb Cordial *45*
    Coriander Vodka *46*

Herb Jellies 47
    Basic Herb Jelly *47*

Cultivating Culinary Herbs 49
- *In the Garden* *49*
- *Indoors* *50*
- *Propagation* *51*
- *Diseases and Insect Pests* *52*
- *Harvesting and Preserving* *52*
    Drying Herbs 53
    Freezing Herbs 53

Classification of Herbs 55
- *Mint Family (Lamiaceae)* *55*
    Basil (*Ocimum* species and cultivars) 55
    Marjoram (*Origanum majorana*) 56
    Mint (*Mentha* species and cultivars) 57

Oregano (*Origanum vulgare*) 57
Rosemary (*Rosmarinus officinalis*) 58
Sage (*Salvia officinalis*) 58
Summer and Winter Savory (*Satureja* species) 59
Thyme (*Thymus* species and cultivars) 59
- *Parsley Family* (*Umbelliferae*) *60*
  Chervil (*Anthriscus cerefolium*) 60
  Cilantro and Coriander (*Coriandrum sativum*) 61
  Dill (*Anethum graveolens*) 61
  Parsley (*Petroselinum crispum*) 62
- *Aster Family* (*Compositae*) *63*
  Tarragon (*Artemisia dracunculus var.* sativa) 63
- *Lily Family* (*Liliaceae*) *63*
  Chives (*Allium schoenoprasum*) 64

About the Author 65
Index 67

Savor the Flavor of Culinary Herbs!

The herb world abounds with savory leaves for seasoning everyday and special dishes. Herbs are essential ingredients for flavoring and spicing up recipes all over the world. Herbs add flavor, character, and uniqueness to recipes. Herbs are aromatic plants whose leaves, stems, and flowers are used as flavoring. Culinary herbs are those in which the leaves, fresh or dried, are used in cooking. Some of the common or basic culinary herbs are basil, chervil, chives, dill, marjoram, mint, oregano, parsley, rosemary, sage, savory, tarragon, and thyme.

Culinary herbs are different from spices. Spices also come from aromatic plants, but are derived from the bark, roots, seeds, buds, and berries; rather than from the fresh or dried leaves. Culinary herbs usually have a mild flavor, while spices tend to have a stronger, pungent flavor.

Basic culinary herbs can be divided into groups to give you an idea of their use in blending with foods. The groups are pungent, strongly scented or accented, and mixer herbs. The first and second group supply leading flavors, while the third group, and the less accented in the second group, complete the blends. Some herbs blend harmoniously with almost any food; others with only a few. Many of the most interesting flavor effects are gained by combining a leading flavor with two or three others that blend with it almost imperceptibly.

The basic culinary herbs that are grouped as pungent, strongly accented, or mixers are:

Pungent

- Rosemary
- Sage
- Winter Savory

Strongly Accented

- Basil
- Cilantro and Coriander
- Dill
- Mint (Peppermint and Spearmint)
- Tarragon
- Thyme

Mixers (especially good in blends)

- Chervil
- Chives
- Parsley
- Summer Savory
- Oregano
- Marjoram

Where do these culinary herbs add aroma and accent to foods? Mediterranean and Italian cuisine often consist of herbal blends that include **basil, marjoram, oregano, rosemary,** and **thyme. Basil** is best to use fresh (when possible) and complements tomatoes, tomato sauces, eggs, fresh salads, and pasta. It adds a wonderful tang to vegetables such as green beans, peas, eggplant, and zucchini. Basil is the significant ingredient in pesto and is an extraordinary complement in both tofu and tempeh marinades. **Oregano** is the preferred herb in Italian cooking, especially in spaghetti sauces and pizzas. It also adds a nice touch in salads, soups, and chicken. Mediterranean cuisine favors the use of oregano as well. **Marjoram** can actually be used as a substitute for oregano, providing a much subtler taste. It often accompanies green beans, mushrooms, and chicken as well. **Thyme** is an exceptional herb for seasoning sausages, soups, casseroles, bread, stuffing, and many cooked vegetables. **Sage**, like thyme, is a terrific addition to sausage and stuffing. Many experienced cooks accent their favorite meatloaf recipes with this herb. Chicken, pork, and lamb taste best when they are flavored with **rosemary**. Adding a pinch to mashed potatoes or peas can add an appetizing twist to these otherwise ordinary side dishes. Take care when preparing foods with dried thyme and rosemary! When dried, these herbs possess an incredibly potent flavor. Adding too much can definitely prove to be a bit overbearing.

Tarragon enhances many foods; among these are chicken, fish, and lentils. A hint of tarragon added to split pea soup is divine. Tarragon also makes especially aromatic herbal vinegar. You can prepare tarragon vinegar by placing sprigs of the herb into a bottle. Pour vinegar into the bottle, completely covering the sprigs. Close the bottle tightly and store for several weeks. This allows the tarragon time to release its flavors. **Savory** has two herbal varieties: summer and winter. Both are often added to salads and poultry stuffing. Bean dishes also benefit from the aroma of these herbs.

Parsley is a widely utilized herb, its flavor being subtle enough to be added to virtually any cuisine. Cooked vegetables, stews, soups, and fresh or prepared salads often contain this herb. As a garnish, parsley adds fantastic eye appeal. **Cilantro,** also referred to as **coriander** or coriander leaves, has an extraordinarily original flavor. It is utilized frequently in Indian, Mexican, and Chinese cooking. Some cooking texts actually identify this herb as Mexican or Chinese parsley. It adds a wonderful flare to salsas and marinades. **Chervil**, like parsley and coriander leaves, is often used as a garnish. This herb seasons soups, salads, and fish. Cheese dishes and potato salads are also excellent choices for the addition of chervil.

Well-known **chives** have a delicate onion flavor, making them a common addition to sour cream and cottage cheese. Sprinkling chives on vegetable stews or soups, particularly those containing eggs or milk-based products, is divine. This herb is placed in many herbal vinegars and jellies. Be certain not to add chives to dishes during boiling, frying, or baking. These processes destroy the herb's natural flavor. **Dill** is another commonly used herb, seasoning sour cream as a vegetable dip, salads, fish (particularly salmon), cold soups, and vegetables. Dill seed is commonly used in various pickling processes. **Mint** leaves are regularly used to adorn desserts, especially those consisting of chocolate or fruit. Mint has a very refreshing taste and is added to several salads and drinks containing fruit, tea blends, jellies, and sauces. Mint jelly or sauce is customarily served with lamb.

This little guide has tips on using the basic culinary herbs to enliven your cooking, as well as tips for growing these herbs so they are available to you practically year-round. It will acquaint you with basic culinary herbs that blend with certain foods, as well as cooking with them. There is a selection of recipes featuring the pungent, strongly accented, and mixer herbs; and recipes for herb butters, cordials, jellies, and seasoning blends. Following the recipes are herb cultivation and preservation basics, including culinary herb plant family classification so that you can easily identify the herbs you want to grow to use in your cooking.

Herbs That Blend With Certain Foods

The following suggestions, which include some of the essential foods and the herbs or herb combinations that go well with them, are given as an aid in selecting dishes for herb accent. There are many possible combinations of delicate and appetizing herb flavors and foods with which they blend; however only a few are mentioned in this guide because you may wish to do your own experimenting after becoming familiar with the various herb flavors, separately or in combinations. Other suggestions and more detailed recipes for using herbs in cooking may be found in a number of books that are available at your local bookstore or library. A list of such books can also be obtained from your local herb society or garden club.

Herbs for Breads

Basil, coriander, dill, oregano, rosemary, sage, and thyme

Herbs for Cheeses

Basil, chervil, chives, coriander, dill, marjoram, mint, parsley, sage, tarragon, and thyme

Herbs for Vegetables

Basil, chervil, chives, coriander, dill, marjoram, oregano, parsley, rosemary, summer or winter savory, tarragon, and thyme

Herbs for Fruits and Sweets

Coriander, mint, and rosemary

Herbs for Salad Dressings and Salads

Basil, chives, dill, marjoram, oregano, parsley, rosemary, sage, summer or winter savory, tarragon, and thyme

Herbs for Soups

Basil, chervil, chives, dill, marjoram, parsley, rosemary, sage, summer or winter savory, and thyme

Herbs for Meats, Poultry, Fish, and Eggs

Savory herbs make possible a variety of appetizing dishes at all times and are particularly useful when economical cuts of meat must take place of those that are more flavorful and expensive.

- **Beef.** After removal from the oven, roasts may be flavored by spreading sweet marjoram flavored butter or finely chopped fresh or powdered dry marjoram leaves over the surface. Grilled, broiled, or sautéed steaks may be topped with butter flavored with dill, marjoram, thyme, or parsley and a little lemon juice, or the surface may be sprinkled with the finely chopped herbs immediately after removal from the heat. Stews or meatloaves may be made more appetizing by adding small quantities of thyme, sweet marjoram, summer savory, chervil, or parsley, individually or a combination of.

- **Pork.** Chops may be rubbed with lemon juice, and powdered sweet marjoram before cooking, and then topped with dill butter after cooking. Fresh ham rubbed with powdered sage before cooking and served with a pan of dressing flavored with poultry seasoning creates an illusion of turkey. Sausage and other ground or chopped meats are usually flavored with sage, either alone or in combination with other herbs.

- **Lamb.** Various combinations of parsley, marjoram, thyme, garlic, or onion may be used. Dill butter or chopped dill leaves with hot butter may be spread on lamb chops.

- **Veal.** Thyme or marjoram is generally used in combination with summer savory and chervil.

- **Poultry.** Various combinations of poultry seasoning made of fresh or dried leaves of basil, parsley, marjoram, rosemary, summer savory, sage, and thyme may be used to add variety to the different dishes prepared from chicken, turkey, and other fowl.

- **Fish.** Broiled or fried fish may have pleasing flavors added by using dill butter or finely chopped dill, basil, or tarragon leaves. Shrimp may be simmered in butter with chopped basil leaves, and clam chowder may be served with a dash of powdered thyme.

- **Eggs.** The many egg dishes that are so commonly prepared may be agreeably varied in flavor by using one of the *fines herbes*—basil, marjoram, rosemary, tarragon, or thyme—for special accent, blended with chervil, chive, parsley, summer savory, or a small quantity of another *fines herbes* chopped or powdered and used as such or in the form of herb butters. Parsley, winter savory, onion juice, and celery tops give a robust flavor to winter omelets when other fresh herbs are not available.

Herbs for Beverages

Hot or cold tea may be flavored by adding sprigs of curly mint, apple mint, orange mint, spearmint, or lemon thyme. Refreshing drinks may be brewed from almost all mints, sage, and lemon thyme and served with a slice of lemon and sugar, if desired. Tomato juice may be pleasingly flavored by adding chopped onion, celery, basil, and tarragon; let it stand several hours for the flavor to develop, strain, and serve cold with lemon or lime.

Cooking with Herbs

Herbs are added to food recipes to supply several unique flavors. They enhance the food's natural flavors or provide extra zest. Consisting of the leaves, flowers, and stems of plants; each herb has its own distinctive taste. When used appropriately, herbs create a livelier, tastier meal; used alone or in combination, herbs hold a specific relationship to individual dishes.

Always remember to purchase herbs in small quantities. Store them in airtight containers to prevent staleness and insect intrusion. Place the containers in a cool, dry, darkened area. Fresh herbs may be refrigerated. Herbal flavors and aromas are released by heat. Culinary herbs release their essential oils at between 85° and 110° F.

Even though fresh herbs are usually preferred, dried versions are often acceptable. Dried herbs can always be substituted for fresh herbs at a ratio of one (dried) to three (fresh). For example, if a recipe calls for three tablespoons of fresh basil, you can substitute one tablespoon of dried basil without losing any flavor. When using dried herbs, select herbs that are as close to whole as possible. By crushing them yourself, you will release more aromatic oils than found in ground, processed varieties.

When using fresh herbs in cold dishes, they must be at room temperature. When preparing a dish that requires a lengthy cooking period, it is best to use a small, tied bunch of fresh herb sprigs. This bundle is referred to as a *bouquet garni* and customarily contains parsley, bay leaf, and thyme. Herbal combinations can also be minced and added to a meal immediately upon completion of cooking, and as a garnish before serving.

When using herbs and spices to season foods, it is important to use them sparingly. Herbs should be used to enhance the food's natural flavors, rather than to dominate them. Remember, each herb has its own distinctive taste, each with specific relationship to individual foods.

8   Flavoring with Culinary Herbs

Pungent

Rosemary

The small narrow leaves of rosemary (*Rosmarinus officinalis*) have a very spicy odor that makes them valuable as a flavoring and scenting agent. Rosemary has a distinctive pine-woody, camphoraceous scent with a fresh bittersweet flavor. The fresh or dried leaves may be used sparingly for special accent with cream soups made of leafy greens, poultry, stews, and sauces. Blend chopped parsley and a little rosemary with sweet butter and spread under the skin of breasts and thighs of chickens for roasting. Use a light touch with rosemary, because a little goes a long way!

Use the leaves, fresh or dried, in:

- Beef, lamb, fish, poultry, stuffings, soups (chicken, pea, and spinach), stews, vegetables, marinades, and fruit cups

Rosemary Chicken in Mushroom Sauce

4 medium skinless chicken breast fillets
1 14.5-ounce can cream of mushroom soup
½ cup sliced baby Portobello mushrooms
4 sprigs of fresh rosemary
Salt and pepper to taste
Aluminum foil

Preheat oven to 350° F.

1. Place each chicken breast fillet on an 8-inch-square piece of aluminum foil. Arrange next to each other in a 13 x 11-inch baking dish.
2. Salt and pepper the chicken. Spoon the cream of mushroom soup over the chicken breasts, dividing evenly among all four.
3. Scatter the sliced mushrooms over the chicken, dividing evenly among all four.
4. Place a sprig of rosemary on each chicken breast.

5. For each chicken breast, fold foil over to form an envelope; crimp edges to close.

6. Place baking dish in the oven and bake for 30 to 35 minutes.

Serves 4

Rosemary Focaccia

1 pound (12-ounce, 14-ounce, or 15.4-ounce) packaged wheat bread mix
4 tablespoons extra-virgin olive oil
2 teaspoons dried rosemary, crushed
6 sun-dried tomatoes, snipped
12 chopped, pitted black olives
1 cup lukewarm water (105° to 115° F)
Kosher salt

Oven 425° F

1. In a large bowl, mix the bread and yeast mix, 2 tablespoons oil, rosemary, tomatoes, olives, and water until it forms a stiff dough.

2. Turn out the dough onto a lightly floured surface and knead thoroughly for 5 minutes.

3. Place in a greased bowl; turn once to grease surface. Cover with a piece of oiled plastic wrap.

4. Let the dough rise in a warm place until it has doubled in size; about one hour.

5. Lightly grease two baking sheets with olive oil.

6. Turn out the risen dough onto a lightly floured surface, punch down and knead again for 5 minutes.

7. Divide into two and shape into rounds. Place on the baking sheet, let rest 10 minutes and punch hollows into the dough. While bread is resting, preheat the oven to 425° F.

8. Drizzle the remaining olive oil over the dough. Sprinkle with salt.

9. Bake the focaccia for 10 to 12 minutes until golden brown and cooked.
10. Slide off onto wire racks to cool. Serve slightly warm.

Makes 2 round loaves

Sage

Sage (*Salvia officinalis*), a shrubby perennial herb of the mint family, is native to southern European countries and is widely cultivated in gardens in most parts of the world. Sage has a slightly bitter flavor that is strong and complex, with hints of lemon and camphor. It is primarily used as poultry seasoning. Use a light touch when seasoning with sage; it can easily overpower your recipe. Use the leaves sparingly with onion for stuffing pork, ducks, or geese. The powdered leaves rubbed on the outside of fresh pork, ham, and loin give a flavor resembling that of stuffed turkey. Crush the fresh leaves to blend with cottage or cream cheese. Combine sage with thyme and use to season beans and soups. Sage contains antioxidants and is a good remedy for digestive problems.

Use the leaves or flowers, fresh or dried, in:

- Stuffings for fish, poultry, and meat, pâté, eggs, poultry, pork, beef, lamb, pasta, cheeses (cheddar, cream, and cottage), sauces (brown and meat), cream soups and chowders, beef stews, and vegetables

Gnocchi with Fried Sage Leaves

¼ cup extra-virgin olive oil
12 fresh sage leaves, washed and dried, any size
Salt and pepper
Cooked prepared gnocchi
1 tablespoon butter, melted

1. In a heavy saucepan, heat the oil.
2. Place sage leaves in oil that reaches 350° F and allow to fry just until slightly golden, but not allowed to brown.

3. Remove with a slotted spoon and drain on a paper towel. Salt and pepper to taste.
4. Toss the gnocchi gently with the butter and serve with the fried sage leaves on top.

Serves 4

Sage Drop Biscuits

1½ cups unbleached, all-purpose flour
½ cup yellow cornmeal
1 tablespoon baking powder
2 teaspoons sugar
½ teaspoon cream of tartar
1 teaspoon dried sage, crushed
¼ teaspoon salt
½ cup butter, slightly softened
1 cup low-fat milk

Preheat oven to 450° F.

1. In a large bowl, stir together flour, cornmeal, baking powder, sugar, cream of tartar, sage, and salt.
2. Cut in butter till mixture resembles coarse crumbs.
3. Make a well in the center and add the milk all at once. Stir until dough clings together.
4. Drop dough from a tablespoon onto a greased baking sheet.
5. Bake in a 450° F oven for 10 to 12 minutes or till golden.

Makes 10

Stuffed Mushrooms with Sage

12 large white mushroom caps, stems removed
½ onion, minced
½ sweet red pepper, minced
1 garlic clove, minced

½ cup crisp breadcrumbs
¼ cup extra-virgin olive oil
12 large fresh sage leaves
Additional olive oil for drizzling
Salt and pepper to taste

Preheat the oven to 400° F.

1. Clean the mushroom caps and set aside.
2. In a heavy skillet, heat a few tablespoons of olive oil and sauté the onion and pepper until softened and caramelized a bit.
3. Add the garlic and cook 1 minute.
4. Add the breadcrumbs and mix thoroughly.
5. Stuff the mushrooms with the seasoned breadcrumb mixture.
6. Pour several tablespoons of olive oil in a baking dish and place the stuffed mushrooms cap side down with the stuffing up.
7. Place one sage leaf on top of each mushroom and drizzle olive oil on top.
8. Bake in a 400° F oven for 15 minutes.

Serves 4 to 6

Winter Savory

Winter savory (*Satureja montana*), an herb of the mint family, is a perennial with an odor and flavor similar to that of the annual-type summer savory, but stronger. It has a peppery spiciness, with summer savory being a little more piquant. Winter savory blends well with different culinary oreganos, thymes, and basils. Even though it has a strong flavor, it does not hold up well to prolonged stewing.

The leaves give an important accent to chicken and turkey stuffing, sausage, and some egg dishes. It adds a wonderful aroma to beans. Combined along with parsley and onion juice, it gives extra zest to French omelets.

Beef Pot Roast

1 2½- to 3-pound beef chuck pot roast
2 tablespoons extra-virgin olive oil
¾ cup water, dry red wine, or tomato juice
1 tablespoon Worcestershire sauce
2 medium red potatoes, cut into quarters
8 small carrots
2 small onions, cut into wedges
2 stalks celery, bias-sliced into 1-inch pieces
1 tablespoon fresh finely chopped winter savory
¼ cup unbleached, all-purpose flour
Salt and pepper to taste

Preheat oven to 325° F.

1. Trim fat from roast. In a Dutch oven brown roast on all sides in hot oil. Drain fat.
2. Combine water, Worcestershire sauce, salt, and pepper. Pour over roast.
3. Bake, covered, in a 325° F oven for 1 hour.
4. Add potatoes, carrots, onions, and celery to meat. Bake for 45 to 60 minutes more or till tender. Add the savory 15 minutes before removing roast from the oven. Remove meat and vegetables from pan.

For Gravy:

1. Pour pan juices into a large measuring cup; skim fat. If necessary, add water to equal 1½ cups.
2. In a small saucepan, combine flour and ½ cup cold water. Stir in juices.
3. Cook and stir until thickened and bubbly. Cook and stir 1 minute more. Season with salt and pepper.

Serves 8 to 10

Ham and Bean Soup

1 15-ounce can navy or great northern beans, undrained
3 cups water
1 pound meaty ham bone
1½ cups sliced celery
1 cup chopped onion
½ teaspoon salt
¼ teaspoon pepper
1 bay leaf
1 tablespoon fresh finely chopped winter savory or 1 teaspoon dried winter savory, crushed

1. In a large saucepan, combine water, ham, celery, onion, salt, pepper, and bay leaf.
2. Cover and simmer for 30 minutes. Add winter savory, cook 15 minutes more.
3. Remove ham bone, and when cool enough to handle, cut meat off bones and coarsely chop. Return meat to saucepan.
4. Stir in the beans. Heat thoroughly.

Serves 4

Savory Roasted Potatoes

2 tablespoons extra-virgin olive oil, divided
2 pounds red potatoes, halved or quartered
½ tablespoon fresh finely chopped thyme
1 teaspoon fresh finely chopped marjoram
1 tablespoon fresh finely chopped winter savory
Salt
Pepper

Preheat oven to 450° F.

1. Use some of the oil to coat a heavy baking sheet or pan.
2. Combine potatoes, thyme, marjoram, and remaining oil in pan and toss well.

3. Season with salt and pepper.
4. Roast until potatoes are golden brown, stirring frequently, about 30 minutes.
5. Sprinkle the savory over the potatoes and stir. Roast 10 minutes more.

Serves 6

STRONGLY ACCENTED

Basil

The common sweet basil (*Ocimum basilicum*), with its several types and varieties, is an annual aromatic plant, widely grown because of its pleasant spicy odor and taste. The leaves have a rich flavor with a hint of pepper. There are large and dwarf types with green, purple, or variegated leaves, some of which are ornamental. Both the leaves and the essential oils distilled from the flowering plants are used as flavoring agents.

Basil is best used fresh as its flavor diminishes significantly when dried. The full flavor of basil is not as evident in its dried form as when it is fresh. The stems and large veins in basil have compounds that will cause it to turn brown and dark, you may want to discard these when making pesto. For easy chopping, use the *chiffonade* method. Lay several basil leaves on top of one another, and then roll them like a cigar. Starting at the tip of your herbal cigar, chop the roll into several small sections. The thickness of the roll makes chopping easy, and with a few knife strokes you can have all your basil chopped in no time!

The leaves, fresh or dry, may be used to improve the flavor of tomato dishes, cucumbers, green salads, eggs, and shrimp. Most other herbs tend to overpower basil's flavor and aroma, but oregano is often used with basil. Other combinations include rosemary, sage, and summer savory. For the most intense flavor, add basil at the end of cooking as prolonged heat will cause basil's volatile oils to dissipate.

Use the leaves, fresh or dried, in:

- Salads, with fresh or cooked tomatoes, with eggplant, peppers or zucchini, in marinades, and in the classic pesto sauce for pasta. The leaves are a flavorful addition to vinegars, lamb, fish, poultry, beans, rice, cheeses, eggs, soups, stews, sauces, breads, or muffins.

- Infused oil, but not vinegar for the long-term. It is one of the flavoring ingredients in the liqueur, Chartreuse.

Basil Pesto

¼ cup pine nuts or walnuts or almonds
2 large cloves garlic
1 cup packed fresh basil leaves
½ cup packed fresh parsley leaves, stems removed
½ cup grated Parmesan or Romano cheese
¼ teaspoon salt
¼ cup extra-virgin olive oil

1. Put pine nuts and garlic in a food processor and process until minced.
2. Add the basil, parsley, cheese, and salt and process until finely minced.
3. With processor on, slowly pour oil through food chute; process until well blended.
4. Spoon into small container and store in the refrigerator. Or freeze portion up to 1 month.

Makes three ¼-cup portions

Tomato-Basil-Mozzarella Salad

3 large ripe tomatoes, cut into ½-inch thick slices (about 1½ pounds)
12 fresh basil leaves, cut out the stems and large veins
8 ounces mozzarella cheese, cut into ¼ inch thick strips
1½ tablespoons olive oil
1½ tablespoons lemon juice
½ teaspoon salt
½ teaspoon pepper

1. Arrange tomato slices on a serving platter. Top each tomato slice with a basil leaf and a cheese strip.
2. Combine oil and lemon juice; drizzle over tomato salad. Sprinkle with salt and pepper. Cover and chill at least 1 hour.

Serves 6

Cilantro and Coriander

That's not chopped parsley in your salsa but cilantro! Chopped cilantro leaves are commonly used in salsa recipes. Cilantro (*Coriandrum sativum*), also known as Chinese parsley, is a versatile herb used in Mexican, Asian, Italian, Indian, and Caribbean cooking. The leaves, stems, and roots can be used in a variety of cooking.

The leaves look similar to that of flat-leafed parsley and the roots looks similar to very skinny parsnips. Cilantro has a sharp flavor with hints of sage, celery, and citrus.

The seed form is known as coriander. Coriander seed has a slightly sweet, minty-lemony flavor. Coriander seed is used extensively as a flavoring and scenting agent, and has usually been imported. The seeds can be used in cookies and French dressing and in combination with other spices; and are often used in Indian and Indonesian cuisines.

The roots may be used in stir fry, or cut into julienne strips and french-fried. They make a zesty addition to Thai cuisine.

Lemon-Coriander Tea Cookies

2 teaspoons lemon juice
⅓ cup low-fat milk
½ cup butter, softened
1¾ cups unbleached, all-purpose flour
¾ cup sugar
1 egg
1 teaspoon baking powder
¼ teaspoon baking soda
1 teaspoon finely shredded lemon peel
½ teaspoon ground coriander seed
Confectioners powdered sugar to garnish
Waxed paper

Preheat oven to 350° F.

1. In a small bowl, stir together the lemon juice and milk. Let stand 5 minutes.
2. In a large bowl, beat butter with an electric mixer on medium to high speed for 30 seconds.

3. To the butter, add 1 cup of the flour, sugar, egg, baking powder, baking soda, lemon peel, coriander, and lemon juice and milk mixture. Beat till thoroughly combined.

4. Beat in remaining flour.

5. Drop by rounded teaspoons 2 inches apart onto an ungreased baking sheet. Bake in a 350° F oven for 10 to 12 minutes or till edges are lightly browned.

6. Cool cookies on a wire rack.

7. Sift a light layer of powdered sugar on a sheet of waxed paper and place cookies on sugar. Sift more powdered sugar on top to coat lightly.

Makes about 48

Salsa Verde

1 13-ounce can tomatillos, rinsed, drained, and finely chopped
1 4-ounce can diced green chili peppers, drained
¼ cup sliced green onion
¼ cup finely chopped green pepper
2 tablespoons snipped cilantro
2 tablespoons lemon juice
1 clove minced garlic
Salt and pepper to taste

1. In a small bowl, mix all the ingredients together.

2. Place half of the mixture in a blender container, cover, and blend until smooth.

3. Pour the blended mixture into the remaining mixture and stir.

4. Cover and chill for at least 4 hours before serving.

5. Serve as a dip for tortilla chips or spoon over vegetable and main dishes.

Makes about 1¾ cups (twenty-eight 1-tablespoon servings)

Steak Seasoning

Ground coriander seeds
Red pepper flakes
Garlic salt
Onion flakes
Freshly ground black pepper
Dried oregano

In a spice shaker, mix equal parts of ground coriander seeds, red pepper flakes, garlic salt, onion flakes, freshly ground pepper, and oregano. Sprinkle on steaks while grilling.

Thai Shrimp with Pasta

3 large garlic cloves, crushed
2 tablespoons fresh ginger, minced
1 bunch fresh cilantro, stems removed (about 2 cups)
¼ cup dry-roasted peanuts
½ teaspoon dried red pepper flakes, crushed
½ cup peanut oil
8 ounces tri-color (veggie) bow tie pasta
Water
12 ounces shrimp, cooked peeled, and deveined
4 green onions, chopped (including green tops)
3 tablespoons fresh lime juice
Salt to taste.

Prepare sauce:

1. In a food processor, process the garlic and ginger a few seconds to mix. Add the cilantro, peanuts, and red pepper; process until finely minced.

2. With processor on, slowly pour oil through food chute; process until well blended.

3. Season to taste with salt. Spoon into a small bowl, cover, and refrigerate. This mixture can be prepared up to one day ahead of time.

Prepare pasta:

1. In a large saucepan, add 3 quarts of water and bring to boiling. Add 1 tablespoon olive oil to help keep the pasta separated.
2. Add the pasta a little at a time so the water does not stop boiling. Reduce heat slightly and boil, uncovered. Stir occasionally.
3. Cook until tender (check for timing on pasta package). Pasta should be tender, yet firm.
4. Place shrimp in a colander. Pour the pasta and cooking water into the colander over the shrimp. Drain well.
5. Return the shrimp and pasta to the saucepan.
6. Add the cilantro and oil mixture, onions, and lime juice. Toss to coat.
7. Divide between plates and serve.

Serves 2

Dill

Fresh dill (*Anethum graveolens*) is widely available in the produce department of most supermarkets. Its aroma is sweet, green grassy, and tea-like. The leaves wilt quickly upon harvesting, but this does not affect the flavor. Just spritz with a fine spray of water, wrap loosely with paper toweling, place in a plastic bag, and store in the refrigerator. The leaves, freshly chopped, may be used alone or in dill butter for grilled, broiled, or sautéed meats and fish, and in sandwiches, fish sauces, and creamed or fricasseed chicken. The flavor of dill diminishes the longer it is cooked. Add it at the last minute for full flavor and aroma. European and American cuisines use the fruiting umbels (seeds) for flavoring pickles, meats, seafood, cheeses, and breads, as well as in spice blends for salad dressings, and curry blends.

Dill seeds are aromatic and warming, and contain carvone as an essential oil, which has a calming effect and aids with digestion by relieving intestinal discomfort.

Cucumbers in Sour Cream

5 large Kirby or pickling cucumbers, peeled and diced
1 teaspoon salt
½ cup low-fat sour cream
¼ cup plain nonfat yogurt
1 tablespoon white vinegar
3 tablespoons finely chopped fresh dill or 1 teaspoon dried dill
¼ teaspoon sugar

1. In a medium-sized bowl, toss the cucumbers with the salt and let stand for 1 hour. Drain thoroughly and pat dry with paper towels.
2. In a separate medium-sized bowl, stir the sour cream and yogurt with the vinegar, dill, and sugar. Add the cucumbers and toss. Season with salt and pepper to taste. Cover and refrigerate for 1 hour.

Serves 6

Dill Batter Bread

1 package dry active yeast
½ teaspoon sugar
¼ cup very warm water
1 egg
1 tablespoon dried minced onions
1 tablespoon butter
1½ tablespoons snipped dill, or 2 teaspoons dried dill
½ teaspoon salt
1 cup small curd cottage cheese, warmed slightly
¼ teaspoon baking powder
2½ cups unbleached, all-purpose flour
Melted butter
Salt

Preheat oven to 350° F.

1. Grease a 1-quart baking dish.
2. Sprinkle yeast and sugar over the ¼-cup very warm water in a 1-cup glass measure. Stir to dissolve yeast. Let stand until bubbly, about 10 minutes.

3. Beat egg slightly in large bowl. Add dried instant onions, butter, dill, salt, cottage cheese, and baking powder; beat until well blended.

4. Stir in yeast mixture until well blended. Stir in enough of the flour to make a soft dough.

5. Place dough in prepared baking dish. Cover with buttered wax paper and a towel. Let rise in warm place away from drafts until doubled in bulk, about 1 hour.

6. Bake in a 350° F oven for 60 minutes or until loaf sounds hollow when tapped with fingers.

7. Turn bread out onto wire rack. Brush with melted butter and sprinkle with salt. Serve warm.

Makes 1 loaf (12 slices)

Dill Mayonnaise

¾ cup mayonnaise
½ cup chopped fresh dill
1 clove garlic, minced
1 teaspoon capers, drained
1 tablespoon lemon juice
1 tablespoon sour cream

1. Place all ingredients in a food processor.
2. Process until well blended.
3. Serve with fish, seafood, or cocktail meatballs.

Makes 1 cup

Mints—Spearmint and Peppermint

There are several species and varieties of mints, such as curly-leaf mint, apple mint, and orange mint; but the common spearmint (*Mentha spicata*) and the peppermint (*M. piperita*) supply the herb and aromatic oils in general use as flavoring agents. Mint has a strong, sweet flavor with a cool aftertaste. Spearmint is the one used principally in flavoring iced tea and other beverages, while peppermint is more commonly used in medicines and confections.

The leaves of the various species and varieties impart their pleasing flavors to tea, beverages, jellies, ice creams, confections, pea, cream of pea soup, and lamb dishes. Mint is predominant in Afghanistani, Egyptian, Indian, and Middle Eastern cuisines and in spice blends such as *chat masola*.

Fresh Persimmons and Mint

4 large ripe persimmons
2 tablespoons dried peppermint, crushed

1. Peel and slice the persimmons. Arrange on a serving plate.
2. Sprinkle the mint evenly over the persimmons.
3. Let stand for 5 minutes for the mint to flavor the persimmons.

Serves 4 to 6

Moroccan Mint Tea

4 cups water
3 to 4 teaspoons Ceylon black tea leaves or 3 to 4 tea bags
10 sprigs fresh spearmint
3 tablespoons sugar
4 sprigs of spearmint for garnish

1. Boil the water in a tea kettle. Warm a teapot.
2. Combine the tea, mint, and sugar in the teapot and add the boiling water. Leave it to brew for 2 or 3 minutes.
3. While brewing, warm glass tumblers (demitasse size or a shot glass size) by rinsing in hot water. Put one sprig of mint in each tumbler. Pour tea into each tumbler through a strainer.

Serves 6

Peppermint Soda

1 cup sugar
½ cup water
¼ cup white vinegar
1 tablespoon lemon juice
3 large sprigs of fresh peppermint
Club soda

Prepare peppermint syrup:

1. In a small saucepan, stir sugar and water over medium heat until sugar dissolves. Bring to the boil.
2. Add vinegar and lemon juice and return to a steady boil.
3. Boil over medium heat for 15 to 18 minutes until thick, skimming foam off the top as required.
4. Add mint sprigs to boiling syrup. Boil for 1 minute, the remove saucepan from heat and leave to cool.
5. Strain syrup and pour into a bottle for storage.

Prepare peppermint soda:

1. Fill one-third of an 8-ounce glass with peppermint syrup, add ice cubes and fill with club soda.
2. Stir gently and float a small mint sprig on top.

Makes ¾ cup syrup

Tarragon

Tarragon (*Artemisia dracunculus*) is a vigorous perennial plant native to western Asia. This sweet anise-scented herb belongs to the aster family and is adaptable to various growing conditions. It is rich in flavor with overtones of anise and pepper. It is widely cultivated in southern Europe for its volatile oil, known commercially as estragon oil, and is used as a flavoring and scenting agent. It is found in many gardens in this country and is used extensively in flavoring foods and vinegars.

It is used in *fines herbes*, *herbes de Provence*, and *bouquet garni*. Fresh tarragon is more desirable for cooking because its flavor components are more pronounced than in its dried version. French tarragon (*Artemisia dracunculus var.* sativa) is the preferred tarragon because of its sweet flavor. Another variant, Russian tarragon (*Artemisia dracunculus var.* inodora) is regularly sold as tarragon, but it pales in taste and aroma in comparison to French tarragon. French tarragon has a glossy narrow, spear-shaped leaf with smooth edges. Russian tarragon looks very similar, but the leaves are more narrow and spiky and the flavor is more bitter.

The aromatic leaves form the leading flavor in green salads, salad dressings, salad vinegars, fish sauces, Béarnaise, tartar, and Hollandaise sauces, and some egg dishes. Parsley and chives complement tarragon well; however it does not mix well with rosemary, sage, or thyme.

Use the leaves, fresh or dried, in:

- Chicken, fish, eggs, tomato juice, steak butters, vinegars, salads, mustards, sauces (Hollandaise, Béarnaise, and tartar), soups (chicken, fish, mushroom, and tomato), and marinades for fish, lamb, or pork

Beets with Tarragon

6 medium beets
1 tablespoon sugar
1 tablespoon snipped fresh tarragon
Salt and pepper to taste
2 tablespoons tarragon vinegar

1. In a large saucepan, place the beets in lightly salted water, cover, and boil until they are tender, about 45 minutes.

2. Remove the beets from the saucepan, cool slightly, slip off skins, and cut them into 1-inch cubes.

3. In a small bowl, mix together the sugar, tarragon, salt, and pepper. Toss with the beets.

4. In a medium saucepan, heat the tarragon vinegar and add the seasoned beets. Sauté for about 2 minutes.

5. Serve warm or chilled.

Serves 6

Tarragon Turkey Breast

5 to 7 pound bone-in turkey breast
1 tablespoon snipped fresh tarragon or 1½ teaspoons dried tarragon, crushed
1 tablespoon snipped fresh parsley or 1½ teaspoons dried parsley, crushed
2 tablespoons extra-virgin olive oil
Pepper
3 medium onions, cut into quarters
½ cup chicken broth

Preheat oven to 375° F.

1. Rinse turkey under cold water. Pat dry.
2. Combine tarragon and parsley. Rub turkey breast with one tablespoon of olive oil and the herb mixture.
3. Toss onions with the remaining olive oil and place in a roasting pan.
4. Put turkey breast on top of the onions, sprinkle with pepper, and add the chicken broth.
5. Roast in oven for 1½ to 1¾ hours or until meat thermometer reads 170° F. Baste occasionally with pan juices.
6. Let stand 15 minutes before carving.

Serves 8 to 10

Tarragon Vinegar

1 cup fresh tarragon leaves or ½ cup dried tarragon
2 cups vinegar, white-wine, rice, or champagne vinegar

1. Place herb leaves into a clean, dry quart jar.
2. Add the vinegar, making sure that all leaves are submerged.
3. Cover with a nonmetal lid or put plastic wrap over the top first, if using a metal lid.

4. Store in a cool, dark place for two weeks before checking the flavor. If desired, let the vinegar steep for another week or two. This allows the tarragon time to release its flavors.

5. Strain out the herbs and put the vinegar into clean, small bottles. If desired, add fresh tarragon sprigs for decoration. Cover tightly with a cork or plastic cap. Store in a dark place.

Makes 2 cups

Thyme

The common English or French thyme (*Thymus vulgaris*) is a small shrub-like perennial growing 1 to 1½ feet in height, a native of south-central Europe and widely cultivated in France, Germany, and Spain for the essential oil that is used in medicine. The plant is commonly grown in gardens for the dried herb, which is used as a seasoning for foods. Thyme has a warm, clove-like flavor. The leaves, usually blended with other herbs, may be used in meats, poultry stuffings, gravies, soups, egg dishes, cheese, and clam chowder. Thyme is a part of *bouquet garni*, *herbes de Provence*, and the Middle Eastern spice blend *zahtar*, along with jerk and curry blends.

Use the leaves or flowers, fresh or dried, in:

- Wild game, beef, soft cheeses, fish, chowders, pâté, vegetables, and tomato sauces

Chicken Noodle Soup with Thyme

4½ cups chicken broth
½ cup chopped onion
4 sprigs of fresh parsley
3 sprigs of fresh thyme or ½ teaspoon dried thyme, crushed
1 bay leaf
¼ teaspoon pepper
1 10-ounce package of frozen mixed vegetables
1 7-ounce package of cooked chicken, cubed
½ cup egg noodles

1. In a large saucepan, mix chicken broth, onion, parsley, thyme, bay leaf, and pepper. Stir in vegetables.
2. Bring to boiling. Stir in egg noodles and cooked chicken; return to boiling, then reduce heat.
3. Cover and simmer for 8 minutes or till noodles are done and vegetables are crisp-tender. Remove and discard the parsley and thyme sprigs (if used instead of dried thyme), and the bay leaf.

Serves 4 to 6

Soft Cheese Spread with Thyme

¼ cup light sour cream
¼ cup nonfat plain yogurt
4 ounces cream cheese, softened to room temperature
2 teaspoons freshly chopped thyme
Dash cayenne pepper
1 clove garlic, crushed
1 teaspoon lemon juice

1. In a small bowl, mix the sour cream and yogurt with an electric mixer on high until fluffy; set aside.
2. In a separate bowl, mix the softened cream cheese with the remaining ingredients and whip until light.
3. Fold in the sour cream and chill until ready to use.

Makes about 1 cup

MIXERS

Chervil

The bright green leaves of chervil (*Anthriscus cerefolium*) look like carrot tops, not too surprising being that it is a member of the carrot family. It also produces characteristic umbels of tiny silvery white flowers at the end of its very short growing period.

Chervil is one of the staples of classic French cooking. Along with chives, tarragon and parsley, it is used in an aromatic seasoning blend called *fines herbes*. Most frequently it is used to flavor eggs, fish, chicken, and light sauces and dressings. It also combines well with mild cheeses and is a tasty addition to herb butters. Chervil is what gives Béarnaise sauce its distinctive taste. Chervil, being a spring time herb, has a natural affinity for other spring time foods: salmon, trout, young asparagus, new potatoes, baby green beans and carrots, and salads of spring greens. Chervil's flavor is lost very easily, either by drying the herb, or too much heat. That is why it should be added at the end of cooking or sprinkled on in its fresh, raw state. One way to keep chervil's flavor is to preserve it in white wine vinegar. Because its flavor is so potent, little else is needed as flavoring when added to foods. This makes it a low calorie way to add interest to meals. Chervil's delicate leaves make it an attractive herb to use for garnishes. Despite this fragile appearance, it keeps well. This herb will keep up to week in the refrigerator when stored in a reclosable plastic bag.

Chervil Pesto Spread

This spread is a tangy alternative to a basil pesto spread and so simple to make, it's especially good spread on fish hot off the barbecue.

1 cup fresh chervil
¼ cup Romano cheese
¼ cup pine nuts
3 tablespoons extra-virgin olive oil
1 clove minced garlic
1 3-ounce package cream cheese softened

1. Combine all the ingredients in a food processor.
2. Process until well chopped and blended.

Makes about 1¾ cups (12 servings)

Cream of Broccoli and Chervil Soup

3 cups broccoli florets or one 10-ounce packaged frozen cut broccoli, cooked
1½ cups chicken broth
1 tablespoon extra-virgin olive oil
1 tablespoon unbleached, all-purpose flour

Salt and pepper to taste
1 cup low-fat milk
2 tablespoons chopped fresh chervil or 1 teaspoon dried chervil, crushed

1. In a blender or food processor, combine the cooked broccoli and ¾ cup of the chicken broth. Cover and blend or process for 1 minute or until smooth. Set aside.
2. In a medium saucepan, heat the oil and stir in the flour, salt, and pepper.
3. Add in the milk all at once. Cook and stir till slightly thickened and bubbly.
4. Cook 1 minute more. Stir in vegetable mixture, chervil, and remaining broth.
5. Cook and stir until heat thorough. If necessary, stir in additional milk to make of desired consistency.

Serves 4

Chives

Chives are bulbous, hardy perennial plants of the genus *Allium* family. Common chives (*Allium schoenoprasum*) have a delicate peppery-onion flavored tubular leaves with abundant and edible rosy-lavender flower heads. Garlic or Chinese chives (*A. tubersum*) have flat, solid leaves with a mild garlic flavor and 2-inch heads of white flowers.

Chives are extremely easy to grow and the tender leaves or the entire plant can be harvested at any time during the season and used fresh. The bulbs or dried leaves are seldom used, since only the fresh plant possesses the pleasant chive flavor. The chopped leaves have a more delicate flavor than onions and can be used with many foods and in many herb mixtures. They are excellent in salads and omelets; fresh and finely chopped chives can be added to butters, soft cheese, and salads. Chives are popular in European and Chinese cuisines.

Use the leaves or flowers, fresh, dried or frozen, in:

- Soups, salads, salad dressings, eggs, dips, vegetables, chicken, soft cheese spreads, butters, white sauces, and fish

Baked Flounder with Chives

4 4-ounce flounder fillets
1 tablespoon extra-virgin olive oil
2 tablespoons snipped fresh chives
Salt and pepper
12-inch square piece of aluminum foil

Preheat oven to 425° F.

1. Place fish on the aluminum foil.
2. Brush with the oil and sprinkle the chives evenly over all fish pieces. Sprinkle with salt and pepper.
3. Fold foil over to form an envelope; crimp edges to close.
4. Bake on a baking sheet in the oven for 15 to 20 minutes.

Serves 4

Chives and Cream Cheese Spread

1 8-ounce package of cream cheese
¼ cup snipped chives

1. In a small bowl, place the cream cheese and bring to room temperature.
2. Blend in the chives. Place in refrigerator for at least 4 hours for the flavors to blend.
3. Spread on melba toast or crackers.

Makes about 1 cup

Parsley

Parsley (*Pertroselinium crispum*) leaves are curly or flat-leafed. Parsley adds color, bringing visual appeal, to many foods. The curly variety is most used as garnish to a dish, while the flat-leafed variety is used almost exclusively for cooking because of it more intense, freshening flavor. The leaves may be used for flavor and for garnish in soups, vegetables, salads, meats, and poultry. The roots go well as a vegetable in soups.

Parsley is a good companion herb as it blends well with both mild and strong herbs, and brings out their flavor. To glean more intensity from dried herbs, sprinkle them over fresh parsley before chopping it. Parsley is prevalent in Middle Eastern cuisine and is popular in the spice blends of *fines herbes, bouquet garni,* and pestos.

Parsley Crumb-Topped Tomatoes

2 large tomatoes
2 tablespoons fine dry bread crumbs
2 tablespoons grated Parmesan cheese
1 small clove garlic, minced
1 tablespoon butter, melted
2 tablespoons snipped parsley
Salt and pepper to taste

Preheat oven to 375° F.

1. Remove stems and cores from the tomatoes, and cut in half crosswise.
2. Place, cut side up, in an 8 x 8 x 2-inch baking dish.
3. In a small bowl, combine the bread crumbs, cheese, garlic, butter, parsley, salt, and pepper.
4. Sprinkle bread crumb seasoning on top of the tomatoes.
5. Bake in a 375° F oven for 15 to 20 minutes or till heated through.

Serves 4

Tabbouleh

¾ cup bulgur
Cold water
½ medium cucumber, seeded and coarsely chopped
½ cup snipped parsley
6 green onions, sliced
2 medium tomatoes, chopped

¼ cup extra-virgin olive oil
¼ cup lemon juice
1 teaspoon dried mint, crushed
1 clove garlic, minced
⅛ teaspoon pepper

1. In a medium-sized bowl, place the bulgur and cover it with cold water and soak for 20 minutes. Rinse bulgur in a colander. Drain well.
2. In a separate bowl, combine bulgur, cucumber, parsley, onions, and tomatoes.
3. In a screw top jar, combine oil, lemon juice, mint, garlic, salt, and pepper. Cover; shake to mix. Pour over bulgur mixture. Toss to coat.
4. Cover and chill 4 to 24 hours.

Serves 6

Summer Savory

Summer savory (*Satureja hortensis*) has a peppery spiciness and is more piquant than winter savory. Its fragrant aroma is minty and slightly medicinal, yet it is warming to the taste. The leaves, fresh or dry, may be added to water for cooking string beans or used in soups, stuffings, and sauces for veal and poultry, and also in egg dishes and salads. This herb is one of the most satisfactory mixers.

Green Bean and Baby Swiss Salad

1 pound fresh green beans, cut in half
½ small red onion, thinly sliced and cut in thirds
⅓ cup extra-virgin olive oil
1½ tablespoons balsamic vinegar
1 tablespoon fresh summer savory, minced
Freshly cracked pepper, to taste
½ cup Baby Swiss cheese, grated or shredded

1. Place a steamer in a large saucepan and add water up to the bottom of the steamer. Add the beans and steam until tender, about 5 minutes.
2. Remove the beans from the steamer and place in a serving bowl.

3. Add onion, oil, vinegar, savory, and pepper. Mix and let sit for 15 minutes, tossing occasionally.
4. Top with cheese and serve.

Serves 4

Grilled Pork Chops with Summer Savory-Mustard Marinade

2 tablespoons Dijon mustard
1 tablespoon red-wine vinegar
¼ cup olive oil
3 tablespoons fresh finely chopped summer savory or 1 tablespoon dried summer savory
1 tablespoon water
Salt and pepper to taste
4 medium pork chops

1. Prepare grill.
2. In a small bowl, whisk together mustard, vinegar, oil, summer savory, water, and salt and pepper to taste.
3. In a baking dish large enough to hold pork chops in one layer, coat them with marinade and let stand, covered, at room temperature 15 minutes.
4. Grill chops on an oiled rack set 5 to 6 inches over glowing coals until just cooked through, about 15 minutes on each side.

Serves 4

Oregano

Oregano (*Origanum vulgare*) is strongly aromatic, minty and camphoraceous, slightly bitter with a mildly astringent mouthfeel. Many grocery stores now carry fresh oregano in the product department. Greek oregano (*O. vulgare var.* hirtum) is the best oregano for culinary purposes. When cooking with fresh oregano, strip the leaves from the stem and discard the stem. Oregano can be overpowering and bitter if too much is used on foods that are mildly flavored, this is one of the reasons it complements meats and vegetables with dominant flavors such as chili, tomato sauce, pizza, zucchini, broccoli, cauliflower, eggplant, and lamb.

Oregano's strong, spicy flavor makes it a perfect match for tomato based sauces, eggplant, seafood, and grilled meats. Italian dishes abound with oregano. Oregano's rich flavor deepens and melds flavors of soups and sauces without overwhelming the dish. Garlic, onion, thyme, basil, parsley, and olive oil are complementary seasonings.

Black Olive Tapanade

2 6-ounce cans medium pitted black or Kalamata olives, drained and rinsed
2 ounces sun-dried tomatoes, finely chopped
2 cloves garlic, minced
1 tablespoon green peppercorns, in brine, crushed
1 tablespoon fresh oregano or 1½ teaspoons dried oregano, crushed
3 to 4 tablespoons extra-virgin olive oil
Salt and ground cayenne pepper to taste

1. In a food processor, place the olives, tomatoes, garlic, green peppercorns, and oregano. Process for a few seconds.
2. Add the olive oil, a little at a time, processing in between additions.
3. Salt and pepper to taste.
4. Let tapanade marinate in the refrigerator 4 to 24 hours.
5. Spread it on crackers or French bread, add it to pasta or deviled eggs, or mix it with vinaigrette for a salad dressing or marinade for vegetables.

Makes 1½ cups

Herbed Angel Hair Pasta

8 ounces packaged Angel Hair pasta
3 tablespoons extra-virgin olive oil
1 clove garlic, minced
¼ cup chopped fresh oregano
Salt and pepper to taste
Grated Parmesan cheese

Cook pasta:

1. In a large saucepan, add 3 quarts of water and bring to boiling. Add 1 tablespoon olive oil to help keep the pasta separated.
2. Add the pasta a little at a time so the water does not stop boiling. Reduce heat slightly and boil, uncovered. Stir occasionally.
3. Cook for 5 to 6 minutes. Test for doneness, pasta is tender but still firm. Drain in a colander.

Seasoning:

1. Return the pasta to the saucepan. Add 2 tablespoons olive oil, garlic, oregano, salt, and pepper.
2. Toss gently until pasta is well coated.
3. Serve topped with freshly grated Parmesan.

Serves 6

Marjoram; Sweet, Pot, and Wild

Let's start out with the fact that all marjorams are oreganos, since the genus name for both is *Origanum*, but not all oreganos are marjorams. Sweet marjoram (*Origanum majorana*) is only one variety of over fifty types of oregano. Pot marjoram (*O. onites*) is another variety, but even this causes confusion, sometimes being called Cretan oregano because of its place of origin.

Three species of marjoram—the sweet, the pot, and the wild (*O. vulgare*)—are used in food flavoring, but sweet marjoram, because of its more delicate flavor, is most commonly found growing in gardens. It possesses a pleasant odor and a warm, aromatic, pleasing flavor.

Whether the herb is oregano or marjoram, both are members of the *Lamiaceae* family, the mint family. Marjoram has a slightly minty, citrusy taste and is most often used in recipes of French or English origin, whereas oregano's more robust flavor is often called for in the recipes of Italian, Greek, North African and Mexican cuisines. Use marjoram's fresh taste to enhance salad dressings, seafood sauces, soups, and poultry. A chicken that has been rubbed with garlic, salt, course black pepper and marjoram, and then grilled makes a quick and delectable summer treat. Marjoram's flavor also works well with cheese, tomato, bean or egg dishes, as well as adding new flavor to potato salad, creamed potatoes, and string beans. The chopped leaves in melted butter may be added to cooked spinach before serving. Pot and wild marjoram leaves have a stronger flavor than sweet marjoram, but much the same uses. Their flavor is excellent for pot roasts.

Marjoram leaves are best used fresh, as their flavor is sweeter and milder. For this reason it is also best to add them at the last moment when you use them for cooking.

Asparagus Salad with Balsamic Vinegar

2 pounds asparagus, tough ends trimmed, cut into 2-inch pieces
⅓ cup balsamic vinegar
3 tablespoons extra virgin olive oil
1 tablespoon Dijon style mustard
1 tablespoon chopped fresh marjoram
1 teaspoon garlic, minced
1 small red bell pepper, cut julienne

1. In a large saucepan, cook asparagus in boiling salted water until crisp-tender, about 3 to 4 minutes. Drain and rinse with cold water.
2. Place cooked asparagus in large bowl and put in the refrigerator until thoroughly chilled.
3. In a small saucepan, add the vinegar and boil over medium heat until it is reduced by half, about 3 minutes. This will sweeten and concentrate the vinegar.
4. Pour the vinegar into a medium-sized bowl, whisk in the olive oil, mustard, marjoram, and garlic. Season to taste with salt and pepper.
5. Add the red peppers to the asparagus and toss gently with dressing.

Serves 6

Multi-Purpose Beef Blend

3 teaspoons dried marjoram
2½ teaspoons dried thyme
2 teaspoons granulated garlic
1 teaspoon ground black pepper

1 teaspoon salt
½ teaspoon ground mustard seed

1. Combine herbs and spices in a small jar.
2. Use for seasoning or marinating meats, in beef stews and soups or shake with red wine vinegar and vegetable oil for salad dressing.

Makes about ¼ cup

Herb Substitutions

Many herbs can be substituted for another similarly flavored herb. When substituting one herb for another, the flavor may not be as originally intended in the recipe. Begin by using half as much of the herb substitute in the recipe than the amount called for the original herb; adjust to your own personal tastes.

Herb	Substitute
Basil	Oregano or thyme
Chervil	Parsley or tarragon
Chive	Green onion, leek, or onion
Cilantro	Parsley
Marjoram	Basil, summer or winter savory, or thyme
Mint	Basil, marjoram, or rosemary
Oregano	Basil or thyme
Parsley	Chervil or cilantro
Rosemary	Summer or winter savory, tarragon, or thyme
Sage	Marjoram, rosemary, or summer or winter savory
Summer or Winter Savory	Marjoram, sage, or thyme
Tarragon	A dash of aniseed, chervil, or a dash of fennel seed
Thyme	Basil, marjoram, oregano, or summer or winter savory

Herb Butter

Herb butters are wonderful accompaniments to grilled meats, fish, poultry, eggs, vegetables, breads, and even poured over popcorn! Good combinations for herb butter are made with parsley or chives, singly, together, or combined with one or more other herbs.

Fresh herbs should be cut finely and blended with the butter. The proportions are approximately 1 well-packed level tablespoon of fresh green herbs or ½ teaspoon of dried herbs to 4 tablespoons (2 ounces) of butter. Dried herbs may be allowed to stand for a few minutes with a little lemon juice before mixing with the butter. Herb butter may be stored for several days in small covered jars in the refrigerator. The butter should contain a dash of lemon juice if it is to be used for making sandwiches or for spreading on grilled, broiled, sautéed meats or fish just before they are served.

Herb butter also may be used with boiled, poached, or scrambled eggs. For a last-minute substitute, place the butter in a glass or earthenware custard cup, add the fresh or dried herbs, salt and pepper to taste, set in boiling water, and let stand 10 to 15 minutes while the hot butter absorbs the flavors. Soft-boiled eggs may be broken into the hot custard cups over the melted flavored butter, or the butter may be poured over poached eggs on toast.

Herb Butter Base

1. Cut up ½ cup unsalted butter and place in an ovenproof bowl.
2. Microwave on low power (10% power) for 1 to 1½ minutes.
3. Transfer warm butter to a cool bowl.

Lemon-Tarragon Butter

½ teaspoon finely shredded lemon peel
1 teaspoon lemon juice
1 teaspoon dried tarragon, crushed

⅛ teaspoon salt
½ cup butter base

1. Combine all ingredients and blend.

Makes about ½ cup

Parsley Butter

1 tablespoon snipped parsley
1 teaspoon lemon juice
¼ teaspoon dried winter or summer savory, crushed
⅛ teaspoon salt
½ cup butter base

1. Combine all ingredients and blend.

Makes about ½ cup

Sage-Thyme Butter

½ teaspoon ground sage
½ teaspoon dried thyme, crushed
1 teaspoon lemon juice
⅛ teaspoon salt
½ cup butter base

1. Combine all ingredients and blend.

Makes about ½ cup

Herb Seasoning Blends

A mixture of herbs, either fresh or dried, placed into savory foods enhance the flavor of the foods as they cook. Well known mixtures are *fines herbes*, *herbes de Provence*, and *bouquet garni*.

Fines herbes is a mixture of robust and mild herbs. It is commonly used in sauces, butter, simple fish dishes, cream-based soups, and egg dishes, such as quiche.

Fines Herbes

1 tablespoon dried tarragon
1 tablespoon dried chervil
1 tablespoon dried chives
1 tablespoon dried parsley

1. Mix together the herbs.
2. Store in a tightly lidded jar in a cool, dark place for up to 4 months.

Makes about ¼ cup

Herbes de Provence is a mixture of more robust herbs to mild ones, with a touch of "Provence", lavender! It is used in meat, poultry, fish, and vegetable dishes, as well of with olives, potatoes, stews, soups, and sauces in French Provençal, or "country-style" cooking as opposed to French *haute cuisine* dishes.

Herbes de Provence

3 tablespoons dried marjoram
3 tablespoons dried thyme
3 tablespoons dried summer or winter savory

1 teaspoon dried basil
1 teaspoon dried rosemary
½ teaspoon dried sage
½ teaspoon dried lavender

1. Mix together the herbs.
2. Store in a tightly lidded jar in a cool, dark place for up to 4 months.

Makes about ½ cup

A *bouquet garni* is a mixture of mild herbs that are dipped into soups, stews, sauces, casseroles, or meat dishes to give them flavor. A *bouquet garni* is made from either fresh herbs tied together or dried herbs mixed and placed in cheesecloth tied into a bag.

Fresh Bouquet Garni

3 sprigs of parsley
1 small sprig of thyme
1 small bay leaf
2 long strips of orange zest
2 long strips of lemon zest
Cotton string

1. Collect all herbs together by their stems, place the orange and lemon zest along side the stems.
2. Tie the stems and zests together securely with a cotton string, leaving a 6- to 12-inch length from the knot. This allows the bouquet garni to be easily placed into and removed from a steaming pot.

Dried Bouquet Garni

1 teaspoon dried parsley
1 teaspoon dried thyme
1 small dried bay leaf, crushed
¼ teaspoon grated orange peel
¼ teaspoon grated lemon peel
Cotton string
Cheesecloth

1. Cut a 6-inch square of cheesecloth. Place all herbs and citrus peel together on the cheesecloth.
2. Gather the corners of the cloth together forming a little bag and tie them securely with cotton string, leaving a 6- to 12-inch length from the knot.

Here are a few flavorful *bouquet garni* mixtures for various meats, soups, and stews. Just adjust the size of the *bouquet garni* to work well with the amount of food being prepared, you want to enhance the flavor of the food, not overpower it.

- Poultry and wild game: 1 sprig parsley, 1 sprig thyme or 1 sprig tarragon, 1 sprig marjoram
- Lamb: Equal portions of rosemary, thyme, savory, spearmint, parsley
- Beef stew: Equal portions of rosemary, thyme, orange zest, parsley
- Pork: Equal portions of sage, marjoram, thyme
- Seafood: Equal portions of dill, tarragon, lemon zest
- Veal stew: Equal portions of marjoram, parsley, onion
- Pea soup: Equal portions of rosemary, parsley
- Tomato soup: Equal portions of basil, parsley, onion, bay leaf
- Stock: 3 sprigs of parsley, 1 sprig of thyme, 1 bay leaf, 1 teaspoon cracked peppercorns

Herb Cordials

Making your own aperitif or after-dinner herb cordial is simple and easy. Commercial herbal cordials are Chartreuse and Benedictine. Choose among coriander, mint, rosemary, tarragon, or thyme for your cordials.

Basic Herb Cordial

2 to 3 cups fresh herb leaves or flowers
1 fifth (750 ml) of vodka, brandy, rum, or whiskey
2 cups sugar
1 cup water

1. Place the leaves or flowers in a large jar with a tight fitting lid.
2. Pour in the liqueur to cover the leaves or flowers.
3. Let steep in a dark place for four to six weeks.
4. Strain and make a sugar syrup. In a small saucepan, stir sugar and water over medium heat until sugar dissolves. Bring to the boil.
5. Boil over medium heat for 15 to 18 minutes until thick, skimming foam off the top as required.
6. Let cool. When cooled, combine the herb-flavored liqueur and sugar syrup.
7. Bottle the herbal cordial and let the flavors blend for several more weeks.

Makes approximately sixteen 1½ ounce drinks

Coriander Vodka

1 tablespoon whole coriander seeds, lightly crushed
1 fifth (750 ml) of vodka

1. Place the vodka and seeds in a large jar with a tight-fitting lid.
2. Let steep in a dark place for 24 hours.
3. Strain and bottle the coriander vodka.
4. Serve well chilled.

Makes approximately sixteen 1½ ounce drinks

Herb Jellies

Herb jellies make flavorful fillings for tea sandwiches when combined with butter or cream cheese, and are a sweet and savory condiment for roasted or grilled meats.

Some popular herb choices for herb jellies are thyme, mint, basil, sage, and tarragon. The simplest base is water, but fruit juice or wine can also be used. Keep in mind that the more of the herbs used in making the jelly, the more intense the flavor.

Basic Herb Jelly

1 to 2 cups of fresh or dried herb leaves or flowers
1½ cups boiling water, fruit juice, or wine
½ cup vinegar (not used when using fruit juice)
3½ cups sugar
3 ounces liquid pectin
2 to 3 jelly jars (half-pint) for canning

Sterilize jelly jars:

1. Wash and dry jars.
2. Fill a large, deep cooking pot, half full of water. Bring to a rolling boil.
3. Place jars into the cooking pot and leave in the boiling water for 10 minutes.
4. Remove the jars from the boiling water.

Prepare jelly:

1. In a small bowl, place the herbs and pour boiling water over them.
2. Cover and let steep for 30 minutes. Strain and measure the liquid, adding water, if necessary, to make 1½ cups.

3. In a large saucepan, add the herbal liquid, vinegar, and sugar.
4. Cook over high heat, stirring, until the mixture come to a full rolling boil.
5. Stir in 3 ounces of liquid pectin. Continue cooking and stirring until the mixture returns to a full rolling boil that can not be stirred down.
6. Cook for 1 minute more, stirring constantly.
7. Remove from heat and skim off any foam from the surface.
8. Ladle into hot, sterilized half-pint jelly jars, leaving ¼-inch headspace. Wipe the rims and attach canning lids.
9. Follow the standard directions for the boiling-water method of preserving, boiling the jars for five minutes.

Boiling water method of preserving:

1. Fill a large, deep cooking pot, half full of water. Bring to a rolling boil.
2. Place filled, lidded canning jars into the cooking pot, leaving at least 1 inch between jars.
3. Add more boiling water to the cooking pot, covering the lids by 2 inches. Cover the pot, bring to a hard boil, and boil for 5 minutes.
4. Remove the jars from the boiling water. Cool, remove bands, label, and store in a cool, dark place.

Makes 2 to 3 half-pint jars of jelly

Cultivating Culinary Herbs

Culinary herbs are relatively easy to grow. The reward of herb cultivation is having fresh, flavorful herbs available at your fingertips whenever you want them! Some culinary herbs are annuals (basil, chervil, cilantro and coriander, dill), perennials (chives, marjoram, mint, oregano, tarragon, thyme), biennials (parsley), or woody plants (rosemary, sage). Some are tolerant to winter temperatures, others are seasonal, or can be grown year-round inside. When buying herbs to plant, check the botanical name to be sure of getting the plant you want.

In addition to furnishing a variety of flavors for use in the kitchen, culinary herbs, because of their ornamental appearance, may be used to add beauty and fragrance to the landscaping around your home. They can be conveniently arranged in flower beds, borders, and rock gardens, or assembled in a small formal herb garden near your kitchen. If they are grown in rows in the vegetable garden, only a small section will be required to produce enough for family use. The perennials and biennials come up early in the spring, and some of them bloom before the annuals are planted. If they are grown on one side or in a corner of the garden or even in flower beds or rock gardens, they will not interfere with the preparation of the garden soil for planting each season. The annuals may be seeded along with other vegetables or they may be arranged in separate beds.

IN THE GARDEN

In general, one short row or only a few feet of row of each of the annuals or half a dozen plants of the perennials will supply enough herbs for the average family. Herbs will grow on any soil or under any system of fertilizing that is suitable for growing vegetables. The soil should be well prepared long enough in advance of planting to allow for settling. Since perennials remain in the same location for several seasons, best results may be obtained by adding compost and organic or commercial fertilizers high in phosphorus to the soil before planting. A mulch of straw applied late in fall will prevent winter injury and will aid in starting early spring growth.

Special attention should be given to the location of a few of the culinary herbs that are sensitive to soil-moisture conditions. Rosemary, sage, and thyme require a well-drained moderately moist soil condition; whereas chervil, parsley, and the mints give the best results on soils that retain considerable moisture but have good drainage. The majority of the herbs, however, may be grown with success under a wide range of soil conditions.

Indoors

A few of the culinary herbs can be grown fairly successfully indoors during the winter, provided favorable growing conditions can be maintained. The annuals mature their fruits or seeds and die at the end of the growing season. They are not so easily grown indoors during the winter as some of the perennials such as chives, mint, rosemary, sage, sweet marjoram, thyme, and winter savory, because new plants must be started from seed and this requires considerable care and favorable growing conditions. Among the best herbs to grow indoors are basil, chives, marjoram, oregano, parsley, rosemary, and thyme.

Bring in the herbs that have been growing in containers outdoors all summer or plant seeds and young plants directly into containers using a commercial potting soil mix. For best results, start new plants in the fall by means of rooted cuttings or by crown or root divisions, rather than potting or moving old plants indoors. In order to make sufficient leaf growth for flavoring purposes during the winter, these plants must have plenty of sunlight and a temperature maintained well above freezing at all times. The annuals and taprooted biennials that are to be grown indoors in winter should be started from seed sown in outdoor beds sufficiently early in the fall to allow the seedlings to become large enough for transplanting before frost. The perennials can be started as described under propagation, either outdoors early in fall or later in indoor containers.

The most important condition for growing herbs indoors is bright light. The plants should get 12 to 14 hours of bright light each day. If a windowsill does not provide that much light, alternative lighting can be a fluorescent lighting unit with warm-white and cool-white fluorescent tubes. Temperature is next, with herbs doing their best at 60° to 70° F during the day and at least 10° cooler at night. Adequate humidity around the herbs is a third important factor. The air in homes is much drier that in most outdoor environments. Raising the humidity around the plants is as simple as grouping them together or setting them on trays of gravel, sand, or capillary matting.

Water the herbs regularly, letting the soil dry slightly between waterings. Fertilize the herbs on a regular basis using a water-soluble houseplant fertilizer, in accordance with package directions.

Propagation

The annuals and biennials are grown from seed sown directly in the garden early in spring, while the perennials generally are better started in indoors in containers from seed or cuttings. Most seedlings require temperatures of 60° to 70° F and bright light to grow well. When the plants are about 2 to 3 inches tall and have developed a second pair of leaves, reset them in the garden at the proper time after all danger of frost is gone.

A few plants, such as rosemary and sage, can be propagated best by stem cuttings. Stems from the latest growth or the upper part of the older stems make the best cuttings and usually can be rooted easily late in summer or early in fall. With a sharp knife, cut the stems into 3- to 4-inch sections, making the cut just above a leaf. Pinch off the lower third of the leaves, taking care not to tear the stem. To prevent wilting, the cuttings should be placed in water as soon as they are removed from the plant.

Plants such as thyme, winter savory, and pot marjoram can be easily propagated by layering. With layering, rooting occurs while the stem is still attached to the plant. Simply bend a shoot to the ground. Scoop out a small hole where the shoot touches, hold the stem in place, and secure it into place with an old-fashioned clothespin or a hairpin-shaped piece of wire. When the covered parts of the stems have rooted they can be cut from the parent and set as individual plants.

Other plants, such as chives and tarragon, can be expanded by dividing the crown clumps into separate bulbs, individual plants, or clones after one or two seasons' growth. This can be done either in fall or early in spring. These subdivisions can be set directly in permanent locations if made in spring or in containers and brought indoors for winter protection if made in fall.

The mints spread rapidly by means of surface or underground runners that may grow several feet from the parent plant, usually at a depth of 1 to 2 inches beneath the surface. New plants spring up at the nodes of the runners during the season. These plants, with roots attached, can be taken up and transplanted in spring or early in summer, or the runners alone can be planted in rows and covered to a depth of 2 inches.

DISEASES AND INSECT PESTS

Fortunately, the culinary herbs are not especially subject to serious damage by disease or insect pests, particularly when grown on a small scale and may be due somewhat to the repellent or inhibitory action of their aromatic oils. When they are grown on a commercial scale, however, certain diseases and insect pests do cause damage under some conditions. For example, peppermint can be susceptible to several fungus diseases that develop under certain weather conditions. The plants of the parsley family (*Umbelliferae*) and dill are sometimes attacked by aphids during the flowering and fruiting period. In unusually dry weather, the red spider mite may cause some damage to sage which may develop brown leaf spots, but since these diseases and insects are of infrequent occurrence and seldom cause serious damage, the gardener does not need to be greatly concerned about them. The insects can be controlled easily with insecticidal soap.

HARVESTING AND PRESERVING

The flavor of the different culinary herbs is due for the most part to a volatile or essential oil contained in small glands in the leaves, seeds, and fruits of the plants. The flavor is retained longer if the herbs are harvested at the right time, either for immediate use or preservation for using at a later time. The young tender leaves can be gathered and used fresh at any time during the season, but for winter use they should be harvested when the plants begin to flower and should be preserved promptly. If the leaves are at all dusty or gritty, they should be washed in cold water and thoroughly drained before use or preserving.

The tender-leaf herbs such as basil, tarragon, and the mints, which have high moisture content must be dried rapidly away from the light if they are to retain their green color. If dried too slowly, they will turn dark or mold. For this reason, a well-ventilated darkened room, such as an attic or other dry airy room, furnishes ideal conditions for preserving these herbs in a short time.

The less succulent leaf herbs such as rosemary, sage, summer savory, and thyme, which contain less moisture, can be partially dried in the sun without affecting their color, but too long exposure should be avoided.

The seed crops, such as coriander and dill seed, should be harvested when mature or when their color changes from green to brown or gray. A few plants of the annual varieties should be left undisturbed to flower and mature seed for planting each season. Seeds should be thoroughly dried before storing, to prevent loss of viability for planting and to prevent molding or loss of quality. After curing for several days in an airy room, a day or two in the sun before storing will insure safekeeping.

As soon as the herb leaves or seeds are dry they should be cleaned by separating them from stems and other foreign matter and packed in suitable containers to prevent loss of the essential oils that give to the herbs their delicate flavor. Glass, metal, or cardboard containers that can be closed tightly will preserve the aroma and flavor. Dark glass jars are preferable over clear glass ones, in that they keep light from bleaching the green leaves. If clear glass jars are used to store dried herbs, keep them stored in a dark room to avoid exposure to light.

Drying Herbs

The top growth and flowering tops of basil, chervil, cilantro, mint, parsley, sage, and summer and winter savory can be tied in small bundles and hung in a well-ventilated dark room or spread thinly on a screen to dry. Cover the seed heads of coriander and dill with paper bags to catch the seeds. Care should be taken to remove all small pieces of woody stems, as they interfere with the use of the leaves in flavoring foods.

After thorough drying, the leaves and flowering tops may be stripped from the stems and packed in containers, such as dark-colored, glass jars with tight fitting lids. Label, date, and store the containers in a dark pantry or cabinet. It is best to use the dried herbs within a year because dried herbs lose much of their flavor or active constituents after a year.

Parsley roots may be spread thinly on screens to dry in the shade and kept as other vegetable root crops such as carrots and parsnips; or sliced and dried.

Rosemary, marjoram, tarragon, and thyme leaves, and flowering tops should be spread thinly on screens and dried in a dark (to prevent them from turning dark), well-ventilated room as rapidly as possible. The dried leaves should be stripped from the leafstalks and stored in a closed container.

Freezing Herbs

Freezing is a particularly effective method for preserving herbs that lose their flavor when dried and for herbs with soft leaves. Basil, chervil, chives, dill, mint, parsley, and tarragon should be considered to be preserved by freezing in order to maintain their flavor.

Freezing fresh herbs is a relatively simple process. Gently cleanse the herbs, blot them dry, and remove leaves from the stalks. You can freeze them whole or chopped, packing into bags or airtight containers. A convenient method of freezing chopped herbs to be used in soups or stews is to simply spoon the clean, chopped herbs into an ice cube tray, cover each cube with water, and freeze. Then, you can pop them right out of the tray and into a cooking pot as needed. Or, you can puree them in a blender with a small amount of water. Then pour the puree into ice cube trays and freeze. Transfer the frozen herbs into labeled plastic freezer bags.

Classification of Herbs

Botanists classify the culinary herbs under several families. The principal families are the *Lamiaceae,* or mint family; the *Umbelliferae,* or parsley family; the *Compositae,* or aster family; and the *Liliaceae,* or lily family. All are classified according to their flower structure and other botanical characteristics. The great majority fall into the first two families named. Learning to recognize the herbs of the different families, which is easily done by observing certain definite characteristics common to all plants of the family, can help you in selecting the most desirable herbal essences to enhance your cooking.

Mint Family (Lamiaceae)

Plants of the mint family have square stems with opposite aromatic leaves. The flowers are arranged in clusters at the base of the uppermost leaves or in terminal spikes. The individual flowers have two lips, the upper ones two-lobed and the lower three-lobed. Each flower produces, when mature, four small seed-like structures. The foliage is dotted with small glands containing the volatile or essential oil that gives to the plant its aroma and flavor. Some of the herbs belonging to this family are basil, marjoram, mint, oregano, rosemary, sage, savory, and thyme.

Basil (*Ocimum* species and cultivars)

Many of the culinary basils are tender annuals in most of the U.S. and Canada. A warm, spicy flavored herb with an intoxicating scent, *Ocimum basilicum* is the main species for cooking. It has dozens of cultivated varieties in a wide range of leaf sizes, colors, and flavors. Large-leaved green basils, such as sweet basil, Italian basil and lettuce-leaf basil, grow to about 2 feet in height. Small-leaved green basils, such as dwarf basil, bush basil or globe basil grow 8 to 12 inches in height. There are basil variations with reddish-purple leaves, which are often used to color vinegar. There are also novelty basils named for their fragrance associations, such as cinnamon, licorice or anise basils. Lemon basil (*O. citriodorum*) is a white-flowered, smaller-leaving plant with a pronounced lemon fragrance. Holy basil or tusli basil (*O. tenuiflorum*) has a scent that combines mint, camphor, clove, and cinnamon.

They are easily grown from seed, from cuttings which root quickly in water, or from purchased plants. They grow best in areas with hot summers, the soil warmed to 70° F, the day length being long and the nights are not below 55° F. Prune when the plant has three to five sets of true leaves to promote branching and maximize growth.

- Location: Basil grows best in humus-rich, moist, well-drained soil in full sun.
- In the garden: Space 12 to 18 inches apart or grow in containers with good drainage.
- Propagation: Sow seed indoors in early spring or outdoors when all danger of frost is gone.
- Care: Grows best in areas with hot summers. Remove flowers by cutting about ¼ of the stem just above the first set of leaves to encourage branching and more leaves. Spray aphids or whiteflies with insecticidal soap. Protect from slugs. Smaller-leaved types are the easiest to grow indoors.
- Harvest: Pick leaves as needed. Pick flowers as they open. Preserve by chopping, mixing with oil, and freezing; much of the flavor is lost in drying.

Marjoram (*Origanum majorana*)

Marjoram is a tender perennial, treated as an annual, growing to 1 foot tall and 6 inches wide, with velvety oval leaves to 1 inch long on wiry stems. It has clustered flower spikes of knotted buds that open into tiny pink or white edible flowers in late summer to early fall. Marjoram has distinctive knotty green seeds. Hardy marjoram or Italian oregano (*O. x majoricum*) is a similar plant.

- Location: Marjoram grows best in average to sandy, well-drained soil in full sun.
- In the garden: Space 8 inches apart or can be grown in containers with good drainage.

- Propagation: Seed can be started indoors, but germination is slow. Take cuttings or layerings in the spring or early summer.
- Care: Water sparingly and trim often enough to keep the plant in shape.
- Harvest: Pick leaves as needed or major harvest just before flowering and again before frost. Preserve by drying or freezing.

Mint (*Mentha* species and cultivars)

Mints are perennials, growing up to 2 feet tall, with oval, pointed, toothed, 2-inch-long leaves in pairs on square stems. Spikes of tiny pink or white flowers appear in the summer. Almost all are very easy to grow. Spearmint (*M. spicata*) is considered the best for cooking. Peppermint (*M. piperita*) is rich in menthol and useful in flavoring.

- Location: Mint rows best in average, moist, well-drained soil in partial shade, but tolerates full sun.
- In the garden: Space 2 feet apart or grow in containers with good drainage.
- Propagation: Divide the plants in spring and fall. Take cuttings in the spring or summer.
- Care: Mint is a very invasive plant, therefore grow it in large pots, kept either above ground or sunk up to the rim, to restrain invasive roots, or sink barriers, 12 inches into the soil on all sides of the plant. Remove flowers to prevent cross-pollination.
- Harvest: Pick only the top tender leaves for cooking; pick as needed. The flavor is much better when used fresh. Preserve by drying or freezing.

Oregano (*Origanum vulgare*)

Oregano is a perennial, growing to 18 inches tall and wide. It has upright to drooping stems with ½- to 2-inch long, velvety, oval leaves. Oregano has clusters of ¼-inch edible mauve or white flowers in summer to early autumn. Flavorful forms of oregano include two species of Greek oregano (*O. vulgare var.* hirtum and *O. heracleoticum*), also known as winter marjoram.

- Location: Oregano grows best in average, well-drained soil in full sun.
- In the garden: Space 18 inches apart or grow in containers with good drainage.
- Propagation: Take cuttings in the summer. Divide the plants in the spring or autumn.
- Care: Spray spider mites or aphids with insecticidal soap.
- Harvest: Pick leaves as needed. Or, for a large harvest, cut back to 3 inches just before flowering and again in late summer. Preserve by drying or freezing.

Rosemary (*Rosmarinus officinalis*)

Rosemary is a woody, evergreen perennial, growing to 3 feet or more tall and as wide. Rosemary has gray-green, leathery, resinous, needle-shaped leaves and edible, pale blue, ¼-inch flowers along stems in the spring and early summer. There are cultivars with pink, white, or dark blue flowers and forms with trailing growth.

- Location: Rosemary grows best in average, well-drained soil in full sun.
- In the garden: Space 1 to 3 feet apart or grow in containers with good drainage.
- Propagation: Take cuttings in the spring or late summer. Use layering in early summer.
- Care: Trim to shape after flowering. Spray aphids, spider mites, whiteflies, or mealy bugs with insecticidal soap.
- Harvest: Pick leaves as needed. Pick flowers as they open. Preserve by drying or freezing.

Sage (*Salvia officinalis*)

Sage is a woody, evergreen perennial, growing to 3 feet tall. It has pebbly, gray-green, oval, 2-inch long leaves and spikes of edible, tubular, ½-inch, blue flowers in late spring to early summer. There are more than 900 species of sage.

- Location: Sage grows best in average, well-drained soil in full sun.
- In the garden: Space 2 feet apart or grow in containers with good drainage.
- Propagation: Take cuttings in the late spring or early summer. Use layering in spring or autumn.
- Care: Trim to shape after flowering. Replace after five years.
- Harvest: Pick leaves as needed. Pick flowers as they open. Preserve by drying.

Summer and Winter Savory (*Satureja* species)

Summer savory (*S. hortensis*) is an annual, growing to 18 inches tall and 10 inches wide, with narrow, 1-inch long, gray-green leaves. White or pale pink ¼-inch flowers form in the summer. Its flavor is sweeter and more delicate that winter savory. Winter savory (*S. montana*) is a semi-evergreen perennial growing to 12 inches tall and 8 inches wide. It has narrow, 1-inch long, dark-green leaves and spikes of ¼-inch white to lavender flowers form in the summer. It is strong scented, which is more piney than its summer counterpart.

- Location: Savory grows best in average, well-drained soil in full sun to partial shade.
- In the garden: Space 10 inches apart or grow in containers with good drainage.
- Propagation: Sow seed indoors in the spring; do not cover with soil. Take cuttings of winter savory in the spring.
- Care: Trim plants regularly to encourage new growth. Apply winter mulch for winter savory.
- Harvest: Pick leaves as needed. Preserve by drying.

Thyme (*Thymus* species and cultivars)

Thyme is a perennial, sometimes evergreen, growing from 1 inch to 12 inches tall, with oval, pointed, ¼-inch long leaves on wiry stems. Thyme has clusters of tiny pink, white, or red flowers in the summer. Common thyme (*T. vulgaris*) grows to 12 inches tall. Forms labeled French or English usually have the best flavor.

- Location: Thyme grows best in average, well-drained soil in full sun to partial shade.
- In the garden: Space 8 to 12 inches apart or grow in containers.
- Propagation: Difficult to start from seed. Divide plants, take cuttings, or use layering in the spring.
- Care: Trim in early spring and again after flowering.
- Harvest: Pick leaves as needed or major harvest just before flowering, cutting plants back to 2 inches. Pick flowers as they open. Preserve by drying or freezing.

Parsley Family (Umbelliferae)

The herbs of the parsley family have small flowers formed in umbels, like dill, at the tops of the hollow stems. The leaves are alternate and finely divided, and the fruit forms in two parts, which separate when mature into two dry seed-like sections. These sections or seeds have five prominent and sometimes four smaller ribs or ridges running lengthwise. These seeds contain aromatic oil that makes them valuable as flavoring agents. Usually the leaves and other parts of the plants contain the aromatic flavor also, but in smaller quantity than the fruits. Some aromatic plants belonging to this family are chervil, cilantro and coriander, dill, and parsley.

Chervil (*Anthriscus cerefolium*)

Chervil is a hardy, cool-season annual, growing 12 to 18 inches tall. It has fine-textured, fernlike leaves and clusters of tiny white flowers in early summer.

- Location: Chervil grows best in humus-rich, moist, well-drained soil in partial shade.
- In the garden: Space 6 inches apart or grow in containers with good drainage.

- Propagation: Sow seed directly into the garden at two-week intervals from early spring until summer, then again in late summer to early autumn. Needs light to germinate. Self-sows.
- Care: Grows best in areas with cool, moist weather; goes to seed quickly with high temperatures and dry soil. Pinch out flower stalks to prolong growth. For fresh leaves year-round, overwinter in a cold frame or grow indoors.
- Harvest: Pick leaves as needed until flowering. Preserve by freezing.

Cilantro and Coriander (*Coriandrum sativum*)

Cilantro is a hardy annual, growing to 2 feet tall with small, open clusters of tiny pinkish white flowers in early to midsummer. It has rounded, ribbed, beige seeds. Mexican coriander (*Eryngium foetidum*) is an evergreen perennial, growing to 18 inches tall and wide in a temperate climate. Vietnamese coriander (*Polygonum odoratum*) is a perennial, growing 12 inches tall, with oval, pointed, 2-inch leaves, withstands hot weather (it favors a hot and dry or hot and humid climate with no winter freeze), and grows well indoors.

- Location: Cilantro grows best in humus-rich, moist, well-drained soil in full sun to partial shade.
- In the garden: Space 6 inches apart or grow in containers with good drainage.
- Propagation: Sow seed directly into the garden after last frost and monthly plantings until late summer. Transplanting may cause plant to bolt and go to seed.
- Harvest: Pick lower leaves as needed. Pick seed heads when brown and orange scented. Dig roots as the plants die down.

Dill (*Anethum graveolens*)

Dill is an annual with ferny, thread-like, blue-green leaves. It has flat, 6-inch clusters of tiny yellow flowers in summer and its seeds are brown, flat, and oval. Varieties grow any where from 18 inches to 4 feet tall.

- Location: Dill grows best in humus-rich, moist, well-drained soil in full sun.
- In the garden: Space 10 inches apart or grow in containers with good drainage.
- Propagation: Sow directly into garden every three weeks from spring until midsummer for a continuous supply of leaves. Self-sows.
- Care: Protect from the wind.
- Harvest: Pick leaves as needed. Cut off flower heads for more fresh foliage. Pick flowers when fully open. Harvest seeds just as they turn brown, cut seed heads 2 to 3 weeks after bloom, and hang upside down in paper bags until the seeds ripen, dry, and drop. Preserve by freezing or drying.

Parsley (*Petroselinum crispum*)

Parsley is a biennial, usually grown as an annual. The curled-leaf form grows 8 to 12 inches tall with finely cut, ruffled, deep-green leaves held on long stems. The flat-leafed form grows to 18 to 24 inches tall with bright-green leaves that resemble celery. Parsley has flat clusters of tiny yellow-green flowers in spring of the second year of growth.

- Location: Parsley grows best in deep, humus-rich, moist, well-drained soil in full sun.
- In the garden: Space 8 to 12 inches apart or grow in containers with good drainage.
- Propagation: Sow seed indoors in the spring. To speed germination, soak seeds overnight in warm water, then rinse well. Transplant carefully to avoid injuring the taproot.
- Care: Remove flower heads to prolong growing season.
- Harvest: Pick leaves as needed. Preserve by drying or freezing.

ASTER FAMILY (COMPOSITAE)

Plants of the large aster family are recognized by their flowers, which are borne in composite heads like the daisy and sunflower. The small individual flowers form on a common receptacle surrounded by leaf-like bracts or scales. The flower head is generally made up of a central disk composed of many small flowers with very small petals or short tubular corollas. Only a few of the culinary herbs, such as tarragon, belong to this family.

Tarragon (*Artemisia dracunculus var.* sativa)

Tarragon is a perennial, growing to 2 feet tall and 18 inches wide. It has upright to sprawling stems with narrow, pointed leaves to 3 inches long and tiny, greenish-white, ball-shaped, sterile flowers in the summer. Russian tarragon (*A. dracunculus var.* inodora) produces seed and is much more vigorous, but the leaves are not as flavorful.

- Location: Tarragon grows best in humus-rich, sandy, well-drained soil in full sun to partial shade.
- In the garden: Space 2 feet apart or grow in containers with good drainage.
- Propagation: Tarragon is a sterile plant, which rarely blooms, and does not produce seed. Divide in the spring. Take cuttings in the spring and summer.
- Care: Cut back in autumn and protect with winter mulch. Divide and replant every three years to maintain vigor. Tarragon does not grow very well in very hot, humid areas. Remove flower heads to keep the plants productive.
- Harvest: Pick leaves as needed. Preserve by freezing or drying. Also keeps well in vinegar.

LILY FAMILY (LILIACEAE)

The lily family is composed chiefly of herbs with bulbous or enlarged root systems and annual stems. It is made up of thirteen subfamilies, each with its particular distinguishing characteristics. All plants of this family have regular symmetrical, six-parted flowers. The fruit usually forms a three-celled berry or pod with few to many seeds. The leaves are generally slender, either flat or tubular, with veins running lengthwise. The culinary herbs of this family belong to the *Allium* or onion group. They are very aromatic, with long, slender strap-shaped or tubular leaves clasping the flower stalk, which rises from a bulb at its base. The flowers are borne in simple umbels, many of them forming bulblets. The most important herbs of this group with flavoring qualities are chives, leek, garlic, and onion.

Chives (*Allium schoenoprasum*)

Chives are perennial, growing to 12 to 18 inches tall, forming clumps 12 to 18 inches across. It has slender, hollow leaves and globular, 1-inch heads of purplish-pink flowers in early summer. Garlic or Chinese chives (*A. tuberosum*) have flat, solid leaves with a mild garlic flavor and 2-inch heads of white flowers.

- Location: Chives grow best in humus-rich, moist, well-drained soil in full sun.

- In the garden: Space about 6 inches apart or grow in containers with good drainage.

- Propagation: Sow seed indoors in the early spring. Divide plants in early spring or autumn in clumps of six bulbs; best done every three years to prevent crowding. Garlic chives self-sow.

- Care: Cut plants back to 2 inches after flowering to encourage new, tender leaf growth; trim regularly where it grows year-round. For an indoor winter crop, start seeds in early autumn or dig a small clump, set in a potting container, and leave outside until the soil freezes, then bring indoors.

- Harvest: Pick leaves as needed, cutting at the base. Pick flowers just as they open. Preserve by freezing.

About the Author

In her previous books, *Building a Healthy Lifestyle: A Simple Nutrition and Fitness Approach* and *Easy and Healthful Mediterranean Cooking,* Mary El-Baz presented an invaluable nutritional program for anyone to build a healthy lifestyle and a collection of savory, nutritious Mediterranean recipes. Now, she now brings you *Flavoring with Culinary Herbs: Tips, Recipes, and Cultivation,* a guide on using culinary herbs to enhance the flavor, aroma, and appeal of foods making meals pleasant and delightful.

Ms. El-Baz holds both undergraduate and graduate degrees from the University of Missouri. She is currently completing her doctorate in Holistic Nutrition.

Index

A

Allium schoenoprasum 30, 64
    See Chives
Anethum graveolens 20, 61
    See Dill
Anthriscus cerefolium 28, 60
    See Chervil
Artemisia dracunculus 24, 25, 63
    See Tarragon
Aster family
    Tarragon 55, 63

B

Basil 2, 4, 5, 15, 16, 39, 55, 56
    Basil Pesto 16
    Tomato-Basil-Mozzarella Salad 16

C

Chervil 2, 3, 28, 29, 39, 60
    Chervil Pesto Spread 29
    Cream of Broccoli and Chervil Soup 29
Chives 2, 3, 30, 31, 53, 64
    Baked Flounder with Chives 31
    Chives and Cream Cheese Spread 31
Cilantro 2, 3, 17, 39, 61
    Salsa Verde 18
    Thai Shrimp with Pasta 19

Compositae 55
Cooking with Herbs
    Asparagus Salad with Balsamic Vinegar 37
    Baked Flounder with Chives 31
    Basil Pesto 16
    Beef Pot Roast 13
    Beets with Tarragon 25
    Black Olive Tapanade 35
    Chervil Pesto Spread 29
    Chicken Noodle Soup with Thyme 27
    Chives and Cream Cheese Spread 31
    Cream of Broccoli and Chervil Soup 29
    Cucumbers in Sour Cream 21
    Dill Batter Bread 21
    Dill Mayonnaise 22
    Fresh Persimmons and Mint 23
    Gnocchi with Fried Sage Leaves 10
    Green Bean and Baby Swiss Salad 33
    Grilled Pork Chops with Summer Savory-Mustard Marinade 34
    Ham and Bean Soup 14
    Herbed Angel Hair Pasta 35
    Lemon-Coriander Tea Cookies 17
    Moroccan Mint Tea 23
    Multi-Purpose Beef Blend 37
    Parsley Crumb-Topped Tomatoes 32
    Peppermint Soda 24

Rosemary Chicken in Mushroom Sauce 8
Rosemary Focaccia 9
Sage Drop Biscuits 11
Salsa Verde 18
Savory Roasted Potatoes 14
Soft Cheese Spread with Thyme 28
Steak Seasoning 19
Stuffed Mushrooms with Sage 11
Tabbouleh 32
Tarragon Turkey Breast 26
Tarragon Vinegar 26
Thai Shrimp with Pasta 19
Tomato-Basil-Mozzarella Salad 16

Coriander 4, 17, 46
Coriander Vodka 46
Lemon-Coriander Tea Cookies 17
Steak Seasoning 19

Coriandrum sativum 17, 61
See Cilantro and Coriander

Cultivating culinary herbs 49
Diseases and insect pests 52
Drying herbs 53
Freezing herbs 53
Harvesting and preserving 52
In the garden 49
Indoors 50
Propagation 51, 56, 57, 58, 59, 60, 61, 62, 63, 64

D

Dill 2, 3, 5, 20, 21, 22, 61, 62
Cucumbers in Sour Cream 21
Dill Batter Bread 21
Dill Mayonnaise 22

H

Herb butter
Lemon-Tarragon Butter 40
Parsley Butter 41
Sage-Thyme Butter 41

Herb cordials
Basic Herb Cordial 45
Coriander Vodka 46

Herb jellies 47

Herb seasoning blends 42
Dried *Bouquet Garni* 43
Fines Herbes 42
Fresh *Bouquet Garni* 43
Herbes de Provence 42

Herb substitutions 39
Herbs for beverages 6
Herbs for breads 4
Herbs for cheeses 4
Herbs for fruits and sweets 4
Herbs for meats, poultry, fish, and eggs 5
Beef 5, 8, 13, 44
Eggs 6
Fish 6
Lamb 5, 44
Pork 5, 44
Poultry 6
Veal 5, 44
Herbs for salad dressings and salads 5
Herbs for soups 5
Herbs for Vegetables 4

L

Labiatae 55
Liliaceae 55
Lily family
Chives 55, 63

M

Marjoram 2, 36, 37, 39, 56
    Asparagus Salad with Balsamic Vinegar 37
    Multi-Purpose Beef Blend 37

Mentha species and cultivars 57
    See Mint

Mint family
    Basil, Marjoram, Mint, Oregano, Rosemary, Sage, Summer and Winter Savory, Thyme 55

Mints 22, 57
    Peppermint 22, 24, 57
    Spearmint 22, 57

Mixer Herbs
    Chervil 2, 3, 28, 29, 39, 60
    Chervil, Chives, Parsley, Summer Savory, Oregano, Marjoram 2, 3, 30, 31, 53, 64
    Marjoram 2, 36, 37, 39, 56
    Oregano 2, 34, 35, 39, 57, 58
    Parsley 2, 3, 25, 31, 32, 39, 41, 53, 60, 62
    Summer Savory 2, 33, 59

O

Ocimum species and cultivars 55
    See Basil

Oregano 2, 34, 35, 39, 57, 58
    Black Olive Tapanade 35
    Herbed Angel Hair Pasta 35

Origanum majorana 36, 56
    See Marjoram

Origanum vulgare 34, 57
    See Oregano

P

Parsley 2, 3, 25, 31, 32, 39, 41, 53, 60, 62
    Parsley Butter 41
    Parsley Crumb-Topped Tomatoes 32
    Tabbouleh 32

Parsley family
    Chervil, Cilantro and Coriander, Dill, Parsley 52, 55, 60

Peppermint
    Fresh Persimmons and Mint 23
    Peppermint Soda 24

Petroselinum crispum 62
    See Parsley

Pungent Herbs
    Rosemary 1, 8, 9, 39, 53, 58
    Sage 1, 2, 10, 11, 39, 41, 50, 58, 59
    Winter savory 6, 12, 59
    Winter Savory 1

R

Rosemary 1, 8, 9, 39, 53, 58
    Rosemary Chicken in Mushroom Sauce 8
    Rosemary Focaccia 9

Rosmarinus officinalis 8, 58
    See Rosemary

S

Sage 1, 2, 10, 11, 39, 41, 50, 58, 59
    Gnocchi with Fried Sage Leaves 10
    Sage Drop Biscuits 11
    Sage-Thyme Butter 41
    Stuffed Mushrooms with Sage 11

Salvia officinalis 10, 58
    See Sage

Satureja species 59
    See Summer and Winter Savory

Spearmint
    Moroccan Mint Tea   23
Strongly Accented Herbs
    Basil   2, 4, 5, 15, 16, 39, 55, 56
    Cilantro and Coriander   2, 17, 61
    Dill   2, 3, 5, 20, 21, 22, 61, 62
    Mints   22, 57
    Tarragon   2, 3, 24, 26, 39, 63
    Thyme   2, 5, 27, 39, 59, 60
Summer Savory   33, 39
    Green Bean and Baby Swiss Salad   33
    Grilled Pork Chops with Summer Savory-Mustard Marinade   34

T

Tarragon   2, 3, 24, 26, 39, 63
    Beets with Tarragon   25
    Lemon-Tarragon Butter   40
    Tarragon Turkey Breast   26
    Tarragon Vinegar   26
Thyme   2, 5, 27, 39, 59, 60
    Chicken Noodle Soup with Thyme   27
    Sage-Thyme Butter   41
    Soft Cheese Spread with Thyme   28
Thymus species and cultivars   59
    See Thyme

U

Umbelliferae   55

W

Winter Savory   12, 59
    Beef Pot Roast   13
    Ham and Bean Soup   14
    Savory Roasted Potatoes   14

978-0-595-37936-1
0-595-37936-2

Printed in the United Kingdom
by Lightning Source UK Ltd.
116983UKS00001B/163